# Centering Moments! Volume II

## Dr. Darryl L Claybon

# Copyright Page

Centering Moments Vol II

Dr. Darryl L Claybon

Copyright©2015

by Darryl L Claybon

ISBN: ISBN-10: 0986236624  ISBN-13: 978-0986236624 (Darryl L. Claybon)

Printed in the United States
For Information Contact:
Dr. Darryl L. Claybon
Atlanta, GA
404-213-6313
drcitc@gmail.com
Cover design by Dr. Darryl L. Claybon
Text Design & Editing Mrs. Mignon Spencer
Graphics by Ms. Rhodia Hernandez
Consulting by Dr. Keith Wilks,
Dr. Carolyn Carter Townsel,
Professor Timothy Moore

## Acknowledgements:

To God be the Glory, the Honor, and the Praise. Just let me live my life And let it be pleasing, Lord to Thee And should I gain any praise, Let it go to Calvary. **Andrae Crouch**

To my family and friends: Thank you for all that you have invested, given, and poured into me. I never would have made it without you...

To my students: Thank you for the moments when the student became the teacher and this teacher became the student.

# Table of Contents

# Introduction

The substance of these pages, in essentially the present form, was given as centering moments at the Interdenominational Theological Center of Atlanta, GA. The centering moments are the meditations used at the beginning of each class. The meditations are reflections derived from the scriptures to introduce the subject material of the lecture for the day. These centering moments are not exhaustive by any means or do they suggest a comprehensive exegesis of the given text.  The intent and purpose is to first, allow the student to settle into the classroom.    Usually when the students arrive for class, they have often experienced a very trying day. Some arrive on "pieces of wood" from the shipwreck, while others arrive "in pieces."  The students that take these courses are hardworking, family centered, faithful people. Their week is full and their day planners do not have enough lines. Yet, they are taking time for theological, philosophical, and spiritual training.  The centering moments give them time to transition from boss, manager, supervisor, caregiver, employee, pastor, priest, chaplain, chauffeur, soccer mom, soccer dad, sister, brother, aunt, uncle, grandparent, etc. to student.

Secondly, Centering Moments are designed to create, provoke, and stir up the gifts and imagination of the readers. Centering Moments provide a safe haven to ask questions and dialogue as opposed to a lecture.  Please share your thoughts. In this type of milieu there are times the students become the teacher, and the teacher becomes the student.  Often there is not enough time in one day to do all that is required in our super high-tech, Facebook/Twitter, microwave society. You may not have time for an entire meditation, but certainly a moment to center yourself daily can fit into even the busiest of schedules. Centering moments are timely and timeless. Centering moments are enduring as well as eternal. Centering moments exist for every occasion.

## Detailing the Setting, the Situation, and the Solution

Consideration of the setting, situation, and solution framework of any particular genre of writing provides a systematic approach to explain what is happening in the text (tell the story). Every story, biblical or non-biblical should contain these three, basic elements.

One can center on a section at a time, or an entire writing. The setting provides some intricate details about the background, the venue, and the actual scenery that is involved in the story. The situation reveals the chaos, the confusion, the mayhem, and often the hopelessness that is experienced by the people in the story. The solution provides the details about how the chaos, the confusion, the mayhem, and the hopelessness are resolved.

Centering Moments are thought provoking, while unobtrusively observing, examining, and challenging when necessary, the traditional perspectives and paradigms of the 21st century.

Centering Moments provide the opportunity for the Self, the Soul, and the Secular, to connect, bond, and unite with the Sacred for just a moment... and in most cases a moment is all that we need. Selah.

Please enjoy your Centering Moments! Also, please feel free to crystalize your thoughts along the way. There is plenty of room between the lines, around the margin, and at the end of each Centering Moment to make notes, so this way you will never lose your thoughts or misplace your notes.

It does not matter if you are alone with

your thoughts and favorite beverage (coffee, tea, water, etc.), or if you are with family, friends, co-workers, or colleagues. May you indeed find refreshment, enlightenment, and sustenance for your journey!

Selah!

Darryl

# Purpose

This guy's walking down the street when he falls in a hole. The walls are so steep he can't get out.  A doctor passes by and the guy shouts up, "Hey you, can you help me out?" The doctor writes a prescription, throws it down in the hole and moves on.  Then a priest comes along and the guy shouts up, "Father, I'm down in this hole can you help me out?" The priest writes out a prayer, throws it down in the hole and moves on.  Then a friend walks by, "Hey, Joe, it's me can you help me out?" And the friend jumps in the hole. Our guy says, "Are you stupid? Now we're both down here." The friend says, "Yeah, but I've been down here before and I know the way out."

Aaron Sorkin, The West Wing

Centering Moments Vol II is simply meant to be that friend that jumps in the hole with you, saying "I've been down here before!" Centering Moments are not meant to be an exhaustive exegesis of the text being pondered. The intention of a centering moment is to create dialogue.

Centering Moment's sole purpose is to ignite the soul and set on fire the "sanctified imagination" of the reader.

Whosoever has an ear, let them hear! (NRSV Mark 4:9)

Pilate's reply, was as mine is, "What I have written, I have written." Darryl

# Centering Moment I

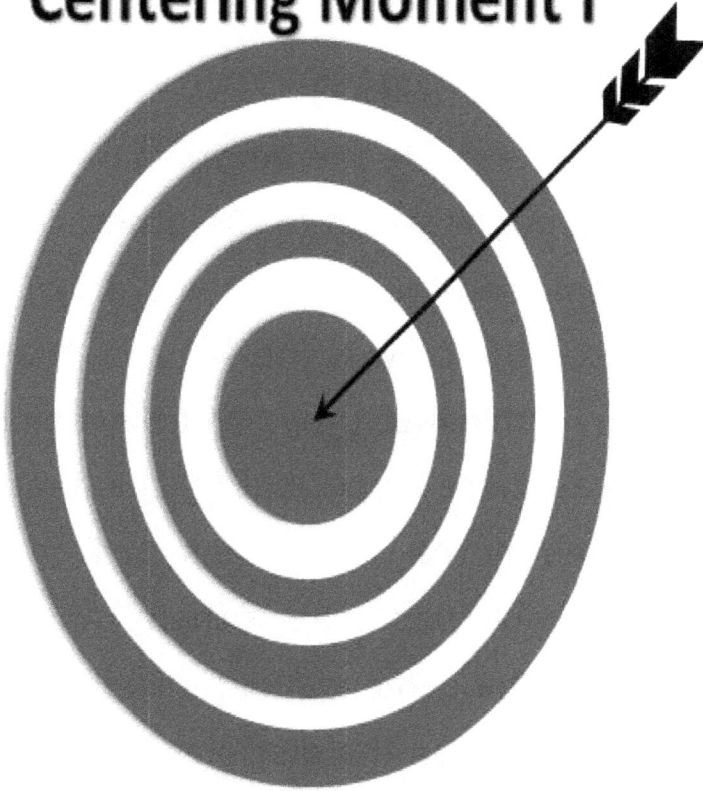

## Centering Moment I
## Dealing with the Storm

Matthew 14:22-33 (NRSV)

"Immediately he made the disciples get into the boat and go on ahead to the other side, while he dismissed the crowds. And after he had dismissed the crowds, he went up the mountain by himself to pray. When evening came, he was there alone, but by this time the boat, battered by the waves, was far from the land, for the wind was against them. And early in the morning he came walking toward them on the sea. But when the disciples saw him walking on the sea, they were terrified, saying, "It is a ghost!" And they cried out in fear. But immediately Jesus spoke to them and said, "Take heart, it is I; do not be afraid."

### Dealing with the Storm

## Setting

In our story, we find a few men facing one storm. These are ordinary men who become extraordinary, because they have been handpicked and chosen by Jesus. They are His disciples. He knows them and calls them each by their names. The call is the same to all of them, follow me. The call today to all men, women, boys and girls remains the same, follow me.

Jesus and his disciples are just finishing the feeding of the multitude...5,000 men, besides the women and the children. Please recall that he takes the two fish and five barley loaves, and creates an "all you can eat fish fry buffet."

However, as exciting, interesting, captivating, fascinating, and compelling as this miracle is, the time has come for everyone to leave. It is time for Jesus to leave. It is time for the disciples to leave as well as the crowd.

It is getting late in the evening and the sun is going down. While dismissing the crowd, Jesus makes his disciples get into the boat and cross to the other side of the lake. The KJV says Jesus "constrains" the disciples; he compels, pressures, and forces them into the boat. Jesus is suggesting that the time has come for them to vacate the premises. The mission for this day has come to an end. Often, many disciples do not know when it is time to leave. Disciples will sometimes get hung up on the miracle and forget about the mission.

However, Jesus says it is time to go. He dismisses the crowd at the same time. He "makes" them leave. His words are clear, crisp and concise, "Let us go to the other side." The time is coming when each person will be making the journey to the other side.

It is interesting that only the disciples received the invitation to go to the other side.

But rest assured, disciple or non-disciple, the hour will come when one must move from this world to the next. Often the move is without our permission and against our will. Many want to stay a while longer; however, when the hour does come, Jesus says "Let us cross over to the other side." What a befitting eulogy for those who have finished their work on earth.

## Situation

They set sail under what we perceive as ideal conditions. Sunshine, blues skies, and not a cloud in the sky. There is just no way that Jesus would have allowed them to leave the shore with hurricane warnings in the area. The crowd dismissed, and the disciples gone, Jesus now goes to the mountains to be alone with God! Jesus retreats and "hides behind the mountains." He is gone to be with the Lord. One has to wonder what the world would be like if more people spent time with God!

However, as Jesus spends time in mental renewal, physical revival, and spiritual resuscitation, the disciples' experience during this time is slightly different. Their situation takes a terrible, horrible, and incredible turn. As they are passing over to the other side, a storm arises.

First the dark clouds appear. After embarking upon this Jesus-composed, proposed, and -superimposed mission, a storm occurs out of nowhere. Perhaps if Aunt Georgia were there she would say "I smell rain!" If Uncle BoBo were on board and looking over the bow, he would say, "There's a storm cloud way out on the ocean, and it is moving this way, and if your soul ain't anchored in Jesus, you will surely drift away."

Matthew says "The waves began to batter, hammer and pound against the boat." Most boats are sturdy and can withstand some battering, but hammering and pounding are something different. They are far from land, which suggests they have come too far to turn around. And now the wind is against them. How can they win?

The problem is further compounded, complicated, and confounded because Jesus is not with them. He is somewhere trying to refill, refuel, and replenish His own soul. The disciples' boat is quickly filling with water while Jesus is off somewhere singing, "My storage is empty!" Remember, when Jesus dismissed the crowd, the crowd was full, the disciples were full, but Jesus left empty.

At this very moment, you might be feeling this same sense of bewilderment. The storm that you are facing is similar to the disciples' storm. The wind and waves are pounding the ship and the boat is filling with water. You might be at the point where you want to throw in the towel. Perhaps it is a relationship storm, a marriage storm, a financial storm, or a sickness storm. It could be a School House Storm, a White House storm; as a matter of fact, it could be a Church House Storm. And the Church House Storm can be either in the Pulpit or the Pew...!!!

Perhaps you feel that "your storage" is empty. That you have given all, you have to give. Perhaps you have spent the day giving to others only to find yourself at home with empty arms, an empty heart or an empty soul.

Please note these colleagues, cohorts and cronies are "commandment following" disciples. They are only doing what Jesus told them to do—"Go to the other side." There is no disobedience whatsoever, and yet the storm still arises. You, too, follow the commands of Jesus with all of your heart, mind, and soul, yet the storm still comes.

At this juncture, it starts to look as though the storm is going to win. It appears that things  are going from bad to worse. It looks as though the 1st century disciples are losing. Sometimes it seems like the disciples here in the 21st century are losing, too. The disciples try to handle the storm, only to discover the storm is handling them.

How do you handle the storm, when the storm is handling you?

### Solution

Thank God, the story does not end here, because Jesus shows up!

The writer says in the fourth watch, Jesus arrives on the scene. That is to say "early in the morning." In the midst of this hectic, frantic, and chaotic moment, Jesus strolls in walking on the stormy sea. The disciples have all but lost it at this point. Most people would have already lost it. They are so afraid; they think that Jesus is a ghost and began to cry out in fear. However, Jesus brings peace, potential, and power to this stormy out-of-control situation.

First Jesus brings peace. He says, "Take heart," I know the boat is filling up with water. I know you feel as though you are sinking. I know that you have been beaten and battered, and feel like you are up that infamous creek, and there is no paddle. But take heart, I am about to bring you out."

Secondly, Jesus brings potential for he says "Do not be afraid!" This statement literally means "stop fearing and don't ever fear again" (Thomas, 2012). Jesus is saying the same to us, his disciples in the twenty-first century: "Stop fearing and don't ever fear again!" Get ahold of this truth, that Jesus is in control of every area of your life, "that He is God." He possesses all power. Then "we can all trust Him fully thru all the storms of life."

Thirdly, He brings power by declaring "it is I." The same "I" that is used when Jesus said:

I am the Bread of Life!

I am the light of the world!

I am the Door of the sheep!

I am the Good Shepherd!

I am the Resurrection and the Life!

I am the Way and the Life!

I am the True Vine!

I am the Bridge over Trouble Waters!

I am the Lilly in the Valley!

I am the Bright and the Morning Star!

I am the Rose of the Sharon!

I am just like my daddy, "I AM that I AM...."

## Centering Questions I

1 Is there such a thing as a man-made storm?

2. Would a loving and kind Jesus, knowingly put the lives of his disciples in jeopardy?

3. Did Jesus ever get tired? Was Jesus' "storage" ever empty? What do you think are some of the ways Jesus can find restoration?

4. What are some ways that you find restoration?

5. Have you been on any spiritual boat rides lately?

What are your thoughts after reading Centering Moment I? Please note, that each time you read it; you will continue to find more inspiration, revelation, and illumination.

1.


2.


3.

# Notes

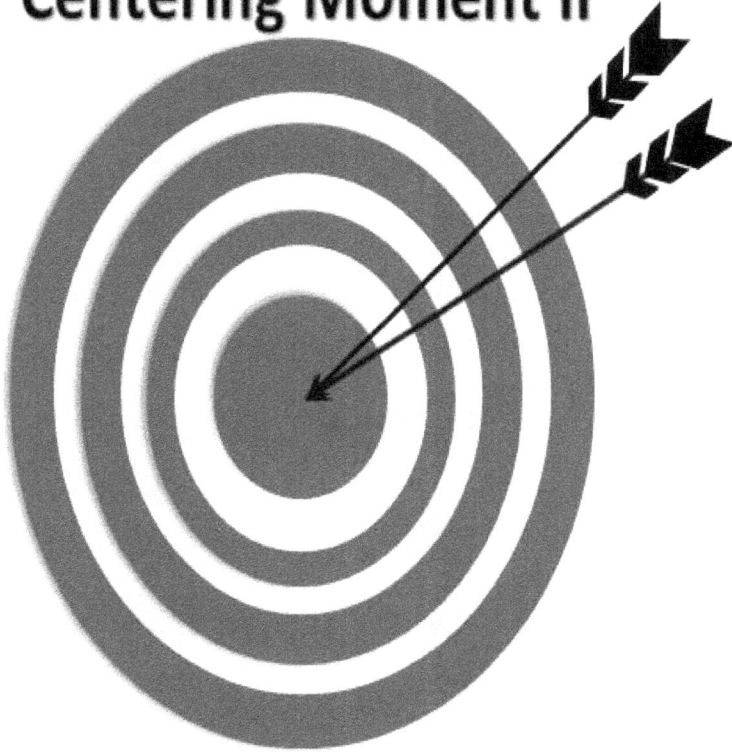

Centering Moment II

## Centering Moment II
## Dealing with the Walls

**Joshua 6: 2-5, 20 (NRSV)**

"You shall march around the city, all the warriors circling the city once. Thus you shall do for six days, with seven priests bearing seven trumpets of rams' horns before the ark. On the seventh day you shall march around the city seven times... As soon as you hear the sound of the trumpet, then all the people shall shout with a great shout; and the wall of the city will fall down flat, and all the people shall charge straight ahead . . . So the people shouted, and the trumpets were blown. As soon as the people heard the sound of the trumpets, they raised a great shout, and the wall fell down flat; so the people charged straight ahead into the city and captured it."

## It's Time for the Walls to come Tumbling Down

## Setting

In our story, the Israelites are facing walls that need to come tumbling down. Perhaps you or someone you know is facing a wall that needs to come tumbling down. The Israelites have come a mighty long way, but still have a long way to go. They are the descendants of Abraham, Isaac, and Jacob.  They have previously faced 400 years of slavery and 40 years of wandering in the wilderness.

The Hebrews, as they were affectionately known by the Egyptians, had crossed the Red Sea and the Jordan River. Their oppressors and their enemies were all drowned in the Red Sea.

The Israelites are now free to enter the Promised Land which God promised Abraham. Finally, a change has come. It was Sam Cook the song writer that offered, "It's been a long, long time coming but a change is going to come" (Cook, 1963).

## Situation

"Now Jericho was shut up inside and out because of the Israelites; no one came out and no one went in" (Joshua 6:6 NRSV).

However, when they get to the Promised Land, the Israelites find a few surprises. First, they find the gate locked. This is indeed strange. Rumors around the camp begin to stir as the Israelites wonder out loud, "Why are the gates locked?" Furthermore, "Who has locked the gates? Who has locked us out of our Promised Land? Where is the key?" someone asked. Surely someone has the key. No one mentioned a key upon leaving Egypt. There was not a key to let them out of Egypt.

God never mentioned a key. Moses never mentioned a key, and Joshua never mentioned a key. The Israelites had experienced locusts, frogs, and the angel of death. Now, at the conclusion of their journey of a thousand miles, their deliverance comes down to a locked gate and no key.

Second, the wall is high. If the missing key is not shocking enough, the Israelites must contend with a wall, and the wall is very high. It is huge in size, and the Israelites have no way to scale the wall. No one thought to bring at least one ladder. No one in this traveling band was prepared for such a thing. At least in Egypt they had ladders! The Promised Land comes with walls and a locked gate. Who knew?

The third surprise is perhaps the biggest surprise of all. Others possess their Promised Land. "What?" they said to one another. "I cannot believe this is happening!" There are people living in our homes, swimming in our Olympic-sized swimming pools, and watching our brand new flat screen televisions.  It is bad enough the gate is locked and the walls are insurmountable! But others who have not sacrificed half the things the Israelites have are living the good life meant for them.

Is God playing games? Is it one of those situations where God says you can look, but do not touch? Eat, but do not taste? Hold for one precious night, but not possess? Smell the bread baking, but you're not allowed to even gather the crumbs that fall from the master's table? For the Israelites, it appears they are a day late and a dollar short! How can God be so cruel? Joe Carr put it this way "You pushed me when I was falling, and would not lend me a helping hand. It's like pouring water on a drowning man." (Carr)

## Solution

Thank God the story does not end here!

Sometimes you have to run on "to see what the end will be...." You must prepare for the eschatological moment. The moment where you see the end!  God knows at the beginning, what the end will be and how things are going to work out. "The Lord said to

Joshua, See, I have handed Jericho over to you, along with its king and soldiers. You shall march around the city, all the warriors circling the city once" (Joshua 6: 2-3).

First, the story suggests that fighting is relevant.  No one gives you anything. In this world, you must fight for everything. You must fight to get it and fight to keep it. Jesus says "From the days of John the Baptist until now the kingdom of heaven has suffered violence and the violent take it by force" (Matthew 11:12 KJV).

Secondly, note that family, friends and church are relevant! No one can go it alone! "Thus you shall do for six days, with seven priests bearing seven trumpets of rams' horns before the ark. On the seventh day you shall march around the city seven times, the priests blowing the trumpets" (Joshua 6:3-4 NRSV). The writer here is suggesting that you cannot afford to engage, participate, or partake in the

"Lone Ranger Syndrome." That is to try and knock the walls down by yourself. It cannot be done alone. Know that the battle is not yours, but it is the Lord's. You must rely upon family, friends, and the church as well. Notice there are warriors as well as priests engaging in the conquest. All play a significant role in this victory. What is needed in this scenario is more in line with the Three Musketeers creed of excellence "All for one, and one for all!" It is hard to lose when warriors are fighting and priests are praying.

Probably most important, we see here that faith is also relevant. "No one can give up, give in, or give out!" Notice in Joshua 6: 3-5 that God commands Joshua to march around the walls of Jericho: "You shall march around the city, all the warriors circling the city once. Thus you shall do for six days with seven priests bearing seven trumpets of rams' horns before the ark. On the seventh day you shall march around the city seven times, the priests blowing the trumpets. When they make a long blast with the ram's horn, as soon as you hear the sound of the trumpet, then all the people shall shout with a great shout; and the wall of the city will fall down flat, and all the people shall charge straight ahead" (NRSV).

Consistency is synonymous with faith. The Israelites are to march around the walls of Jericho one time. They are to do this for six days with each day becoming more controversial than the day before. No doubt some were wondering why just one time each day. The hitching and unhitching of the horses, equipment, and carriages was indeed tedious. Imagine each warrior at sunrise putting on all of that equipment every day for what must have felt like for naught, for zero, or for nothing. One has to wonder just what exactly is being proven here?

The seven priests are present with them. The daily praying, meditating, and carrying out the very strict Deuteronomist rituals was not a time for error due to human fatigue or human failure. The Israelites are duty bound to pray for something that has not yet happened, but obligated to pray as though it has happened. However, they must not give in, give up, or give out!

Finally on the seventh day, they are to march around the city seven times while the priests blow their trumpets. Then and only then are the people to shout with a great shout. At this point the wall of the city will fall down flat, tumble if you will. All the people shall charge straight ahead.

Joshua fought the battle of Jericho, and the walls came tumbling down!

## Centering Questions II

1. Who locked the gates at Jericho?

2. Why are there no keys or ladders provided?

3. Who are the inhabitants of Jericho before the Israelites arrive?

4. Why is this not discussed from the beginning? Is there someone living in your promised land?

5. Is it fair for the citizens of Jericho to lose their land to the Israelites?

What are your thoughts after reading Centering Moment II? Please note, that each time you read it; you will continue to find more inspiration, revelation, and illumination.

1.

2.

3.

# Notes

# Centering Moment III

# Centering Moments III
# Dealing with Thorns
### Corinthians 12:2-9 (NRSV)

And I know that such a person—whether in the body or out of the body I do not know; God knows— was caught up into Paradise and heard things that are not to be told, that no mortal is permitted to repeat. On behalf of such a one I will boast, but on my own behalf I will not boast, except of my weaknesses.

Therefore, to keep me from being too elated, a thorn was given me in the flesh, a messenger of Satan to torment me, to keep me from being too elated. Three times I appealed to the Lord about this, that it would leave me, but he said to me, "My grace is sufficient for you, for power is made perfect in weakness.

**A Problem that will not go Away!**

# Setting

In our story, the Apostle Paul is dealing with a problem that will not go away. According to his testimony, the Apostle Paul was personally handpicked, chosen and ordained by the Lord Jesus Christ. Biblically, an apostle was someone who interacted with Jesus or personally knew Jesus before his crucifixion and after his crucifixion (Slick, 2014). However, Paul is not included in the calling of the original twelve.

Paul is famous for what God did to him as well as what Paul did for Jesus. Paul's calling and conversion actually comes after the Resurrection of Jesus. Paul claims that one night while he was on the road to Damascus, Jesus literally knocked the hell out of him! He was on his way to persecute more Christians when Jesus knocked him from his beast. Paul declares while he was down on the ground that he saw a bright light shining brighter than the noonday sun, and a voice asking, "Why persecutes thou me?" Paul's reply is "Who art Thou?" and Jesus says "I am the Lord Jesus Christ" (Acts 9:4). Paul declares that Jesus put him on the road called Straight.

Here in the 12th chapter of 2 Corinthians, Paul goes on to talk about being caught up to the third heaven. He is not sure whether he is in the body or if this is a spiritual manifestation. He declares "I do not know, but God knows." He does know he is caught up into Paradise and hears things that no mortal is permitted to repeat.

In a world that appears to have gone crazy, it would be wonderful to know what Paul has seen and heard. Perhaps he could speak to this present age and help us reach our fullest potential as human beings. As opposed to our experience of the daily threat of cyber wars, nuclear annihilation and unrelenting degradation toward each other;

while at the same time, we are racing toward our utter destruction.

Paul was called, converted, and allowed to look over into Paradise. Here in the 21st century we can only imagine what Paradise may have looked like to him. The advancement of the computer, the Internet, and smartphone is showing us a world that Paul could not have imagined. Our opportunities are boundless, so for us Paradise will be something to behold. If the secular world has this much-unbridled possibility, the sacred should be as Paul said—to hear and see things that no mortal should repeat!

## Situation

Through this vivid, theatrical, and melodramatic episode, it appears that Paul has it all together. He is personally handpicked, chosen and ordained by the Lord Jesus Christ. He is secure, sure and confident of his calling, his mission and his ministry. It would seem with such a hands-on-approach and hands-on encounter with Jesus that Paul's life would move into that place called "Happily Ever After." However, with all that he has seen, heard, and experienced, Paul still has one problem that will not go away!

Paul offers: "Therefore, to keep[a] me from being too elated, a thorn was given me in the flesh, a messenger of Satan to torment me, to keep me from being too elated.[b] 8 Three times I appealed to the Lord about this, that it would leave me" (2 Corinth NRSV)

He is saying that he has a situation or circumstance that has no resolution. Scholars and theologians alike cannot agree on what exactly was Paul's ailment. It appears to have been physical in nature but most certainly could have been spiritual. Paul equates the ailment to a thorn in the flesh. Thorns have spikes, and sharp barb-like projections, which pricks a painful, gaping, bleeding hole in the muscle going in; then tears, rips, and gashes the flesh coming out.

Some suggest that perhaps Paul's thorn was an eye ailment. In some of the Pauline letters, from time to time, when Paul did the actual writing, some of the writings were in large letters, indicating the inability to see as well as needed (Wommack, 2015). Other theories suggest Paul's thorn was a skin rash of such proportions that it affected his ability to do public ministry. The people to whom Paul is ministering pay more attention to his malady than his ministry. Again, one thing is sure, it irritates Paul so badly; all he understands is there is a thorn in my flesh (William, n.d.).

Paul's thorn is purposeful, persistent, and relentless. It is used to keep Paul from becoming too elated, too high, or too thrilled with himself. He further describes this uncomfortable, painful and sore malady as a messenger of Satan sent to torment him. The KJV uses the word buffet instead of torment (NRSV). The Greek translation for the word is "kolaphizō" [ko-lä-fē'-zō] which means to slap around or strike with a blow (Greek Lexicon). Perhaps someone today is feeling the effects of being buffeted right now. A continual slapping around or slapping upside the head and it will not stop. It continues 24 hours a day, 7 days a week and 365 days of every year.

Paul decided that prayer will fix his ailment. So he prays, he appeals, and he seeks the Lord. Perhaps reminding himself that "if God is for us, then who shall be against us" (Romans 8:31). Perhaps Paul calls upon the promise that "No weapon formed against me, shall prosper" (Isaiah 54:17). Or perhaps he proclaims, "Lord you are the author and the finisher of our faith, whatever you start, you can finish!" (Hebrews 12:2).

However, it was to no avail, Jesus does not respond. How can the Lord who can knock the hell out of him (spiritually speaking), not have the power to knock this ailment from his body? Perhaps you, too, are wondering why you were saved from the fire, only to be swallowed by the floods?

## Solution

So how does this story speak to us today, here in the 21st century and beyond? What then shall we say to these things?

First, thorns are pointy and painful. Obviously, Paul is experiencing a great deal of anguish. He is trying to handle the problem, but it seems the problem is handling him. Perhaps you are feeling overwhelmed by the vicissitudes of life, up one day and down the next. The recurring problem may appear more than you can bear, and all that is wanted and needed is just a small amount of relief.

Second, thorns are problematic. Perhaps one of the reasons Paul wants to rid himself of this problem is because it is interfering with his life and his ability to effectively minister. Perhaps he surmises that if the Lord would just move this "one mountain" then he could continue his missionary journey in peace.

Third, some thorns will not go away. The Apostle Paul prayed with all of his heart and soul for his ailment to be taken away. However, he does not get the answer he is expecting. He gets a better response. The Lord tells Paul that this particular thorn is going to stay. It is not going anywhere.

Nevertheless, the Lord also assures Paul that:

My Grace is sufficient!

My Grace is appropriate!

My Grace is abundant.

My Grace is adequate!

My Grace is enough!

My Grace is all that you need!

## Centering Question III

1. What was Paul doing before being called by Jesus?

2. Is Paul's former occupation considered a "Spirit of Evil" or "Full of Hell?"

3. What do you think is Paul's thorn?

4. Does everyone have a thorn or a problem that will not go away?

5. What about you?

What are your thoughts after reading Centering Moment III? Please note, that each time you read it; you will continue to find more inspiration, revelation, and illumination.

1.

2.

3.

# Notes

# Notes

Centering Moment IV

# CENTERING MOMENTS IV
# DEALING WITH DEPRESSION

Psalm 3:1-3 (KJV) A Psalm of David, when he fled from his son Absalom. "Lord, how are they increased that trouble me? Many are they that rise up against me. Many there be which say of my soul, There is no help for him in God. Selah. But thou, O Lord, art a shield for me; my glory, and the lifter up of mine head."

## DEALING WITH DEPRESSION

# Setting

In our story, King David is dealing with depression. The same King David that wrote Psalm 23: "The Lord is my shepherd, and I shall not want. He makes me to lie down in green pastures and leads me beside the still waters," also wrote Psalm 3. In Psalm 23, David goes on to say, "Yea, though I walk through the valley of the shadow of death, I will fear no evil: for thou art with me; thy rod and thy staff they comfort me and I shall dwell in the house of the Lord forever." The same King David that said "This is the day, the Lord has made, and I shall be glad in it" also speaks the depressing words of Psalm 3.

On this particular day, King David is dealing with the vicissitudes of life. Vicissitudes means "the changes, variations, and fluctuations of life" (Mish, 2002). In other words, David is dealing with the ups and downs of life. At this juncture, he is a long way from being up! The King of Israel is hiding in a cave. Often depression is described by some as a deep dark hole or tunnel with no light at the end. It gets deeper and darker with no way out.

We cannot be exactly sure what is driving David to this point. What is the trigger or what are the triggers that prompt David's spiral into this episode of depression? Scholars and theologians seem to believe that David's visit into the abyss is driven by familial implications.

One of the obvious triggers appears to be his relationship with his son Absalom. His son has made a declaration. Absalom said, "When I see my daddy, I am going to kill him." His anger towards David had reached a point of no return. This kind of anger is understood when it comes from a stranger or an enemy.

However, Absalom is David's flesh and blood! This is David's son. This scenario begs the question "How can you love someone who is trying to kill you?"

Another trigger seems to be the continual degradation, collapse, and breakdown of David's family. Tamera, David's daughter, was attacked by her brother, another one of David's son. Again, not by an enemy or stranger, but a horrific deed inculcated and carried out by the next of kin. David no doubt hearing the words of the prophet echoing in his ears, "The sword shall never leave your house" (2 Sam 12:10).

One final trigger may be the wrestling match between David and David's own demons. There are times when the greatest enemy is the "enemy that is in me!" They are inside of David, an internal and eternal struggle that has probably existed since his childhood or even at birth. David's sense of privilege and God's gift of freewill suggests to him that he can have anything he wants. Even if what he wants belongs to another man.

Freewill offers that one can have whatever one wants. However, one must determine if what one wants is what one needs. "Surely it is better to want and not have," than to "have and not want what one has." David's unmitigated desires have led him to premeditated murder in the first degree. He can have Bathsheba, but it comes with something David does not want or need—the expense of an innocent man's life and the breaking of God's law, "Thou shalt not kill."

## Situation

There are three things that suggest that David may be in a state of depression. First, while hiding in this cave, David feels that the whole world is against him. In Psalm 3:1, David laments, "Lord, how they are increased that trouble me! Many are they that rise up against me." David feels that he does not have a friend anywhere. In David's mind, there appears to be an increase in the number of people that are troubling him, upsetting him, and stressing him out. Many means "numerous, voluminous, and countless" are those that rise up against David and that number appears to grow every day.

The second sign that David is becoming somewhat delusional is he hears voices. "Many there be which say of my soul" suggests that David is overhearing conversations. This may be true in the sense that he actually heard the conversations. However, real or imagined, in his mind, "many" are now talking about him. Many have risen up against him, and he is the subject of their conversations. In the cave, he is recanting these conversations and feels that everyone is talking about him.

Third, it appears that David is now making a play on God. He is suggesting that many are saying that there is no help for David, even in God. In other words, in this conversation David is saying that not even you Lord can help me! David offers that he messed things up so badly that even the Almighty Lord God cannot change it. There are many today who feel their situation is so bad that even God cannot bring them out. Some may feel as the blues writer who says, "I've been down so long, you know down don't bother me" (King, 1967). Others perhaps may feel as the country music writer says, "I don't know if I am getting better, or just getting used to the pain" (Lawrence, 1994). The R & B music writer would offer "it makes me want to holler and throw up both my hands" (Gaye, 1971). The Hip-hop generation would suggest "It's like a jungle sometimes, it makes me wonder, how I keep from going under" (Grand Master Flash, 1982).

## Solution

But thank the Lord; the story does not end here. Please notice at the end of verse two, there is the word "Selah." Selah is not so much a spoken word as much as it is an instruction. For the singer, Selah means "rest or pause, take a deep breath, and relax your voice, throat, and windpipes at this juncture in the song." For the psalmist, it means the same, rest, pause, and look up! "But thou, O Lord, art a shield for me; my glory, and the lifter up of mine head" (Psalm 3:3).

David says after resting, pausing and looking up, "But Thou oh Lord." It is here that David begins to look to the hills from whence comes his help. If you are struggling today, trying to keep your head above water, pause, rest, and look up. Reminding yourself of the same three things that David reminds himself of about the Lord.

First, he says "Thou art a shield for me." A shield is an apparatus used by those engaged in battle to protect themselves. The shield is used as a deflector, a reflector, and a protector.

Secondly, David laments, "Lord you are my glory." David is suggesting, I am not living for my own glory, but I'm living to glorify your name. No wonder the gospel song writer said "I am singing glory to his name, precious name." (Elisha A. Hoffman, *pub.*1878)

Thirdly, David writes "You are the lifter up of my head." I may have a bowed down head and a heavy heart, but Lord you will not allow me to walk around too long with a bowed down head. You are the lifter, the crane, the winch, the hoist, the crank and the pulley, which lifts my head.

# Centering Questions IV

1. Explain: "Surely it is better to want and not have," than to "have and not want what one has."

2. Why do you think David feels that he can have what he wants?

3. What is free will?

4. Why is it important to consider the consequences of free will?

5. Will everyone have moments of doubt and depression, even if their walk with the Lord is a very close walk?

What are your thoughts after reading Centering Moment IV? Please note, that each time you read it; you will continue to find more inspiration, revelation, and illumination.

1.


2.



3.

# Notes

## Bibliography/References

Cahill, Lisa Sowle. Families: A Christian Social Perspective.  Minneapolis, MN: Fortress Press, 2000..

Carr, J. (n.d) Pouring Water on a Drowning Man. Retrieved from
http://www.lyricsmode.com/lyrics/j/jameCarr, J/pouring_water_on_a_drowning_m an.html#!

Chance, J. Bradley.  "Luke 15: Seeking the Outsiders."  Review & Expositor (Spring 1994).

Chimmarusti, Rocco A. and Jay Lappin.  "Beginning Family Therapy."  Family Therapy Collections, no. 14  (1985)..

Claybon, Darryl, L. Lessons from the Jericho Road. (2011). Dante Publishing. Atlanta, GA Cook, S (n.d.)

Cook, Sam: A change is gonna come! Retrieved from http://www.songfacts.com/ detail .php?id= 3673  (1963)

Crouch, Andre. To God be the Glory.(1971)
    Retrieved from
    http://www.allthelyrics.com/lyrics/andrae
    crouch/to_god_be_the_glory-lyrics-3

Dash, Michael I.N., Jonathan Jackson, and
    Stephen C. Rasor. Hidden Wholeness: An
    African American Spirituality for Individuals
    and Communities. Cleveland, OH: United
    Church Press, 1997.

Erickson, E. H. Childhood and Society.  New
    York: Norton, 1950.

Farrugia, David.  "Selfishness, Greed, and
    Counseling."  In Counseling & Values, vol.
    46 (January 2002).

Foss, Mike, and Terri Elton.  What Really
    Matters: 30 Devotions for Church
    Leadership Teams.  Loveland, CO:  Group
    Publishing, 2003.

Felluga, Dino.  "Modules on Freud:  On
    Psychosexual Development, 1885"
    Introductory Guide to Critical Theory.
    (Purdue University)  Retrieved from
    http://www.purdue.edu/guidetotheory/ps
    ychoanalysis/freud.html;

Gaye, Marvin. (1971) Inner City Blues (Make Me Want to Holler) Retrieved from hhttp://www.songfacts.com/detail.php?id=105 03

Grand Master Flash. (1982)The Message. Retrieved from http://www.metrolyrics .com/the- message-lyrics-grandmaster -flash.html

Greek Lexicon :: G2852 (KJV). Retrieved from http://www.blueletterbible.org/ lang/lexicon/le xicon.cfm?Strongs =G2852&t=KJV

Hedgy, James. "Look in the Lost and Found." Family & Life, no. 185 (2001).

Hedrick, Charles W. "Prolegomena to Reading Parables: Luke 13: 6-9 as a Test Case." Review and Expositor, no. 94 (1997).

Hill, ZZ, LaSalle, Denise. Steppin out, Steppin in. (1995) Retrieved from http://www.cduni verse.com/ search/xx/m usic/pid/1062935/

Hidden Wholeness: An African American Spirituality for Individuals and Communities. 1997 Cleveland, OH: United Church Press Jackson, Thomas, ed.

The Works of the Rev. John Wesley, 14 vols. (1831) reprint, Grand Rapids, MI: Baker, 1979.

King, Albert. (1967) Down Don't Bother Me. Retrieved fromhttp://www.metrolyrics. com/down-don-t- bother-me-lyrics-albert-king.html

Lao-tzu, The Way of Lao-tzu Chinese philosopher (60 BC - 531 BC.( 2003) C Penguin Group (USA) Retrieved from http://www.quotationspage.com/quotes/Laotz

Lawrence, Tracy. (2013) Getting Used to the Pain. Retrieved from http://www.cow boy lyrics.com/lyrics/lawrence-tracy/used-to-the-pain-16158.html

Kreeft, Peter/ Dougherty, Trent, Socratic Logic. (2010)St Augustine Pr Inc, South Bend, IN.

Matthew Henry, Commentary, Vol. 5, McLean,
    VA:  MacDonald Publishing Company,
    1996. Mish, Frederick C. ed. Merriam-
    Webster's

Collegiate Dictionary, 10th ed. Springfield, MA:
    Merriam-Webster, Incorporated, 2002.

Robertson, Anita.  Learning While
    Leading:  Increasing Your Effectiveness In
    Ministry.  New York, NY:The Alban
    Institute, 2000.


Rothauge, Arlin J. The Life Cycle in
    Congregations: A Process of Natural
    Creation and an Opportunity for a New
    Creation. Retrieved from
    http://www.ecusa.anglican.org/
    documents/life-cycle.pdf, Internet.

Schleiermacher, Friedrich D. E.  Absolute
    Dependence.  1821:  English translation of
    2nd ed Retrieved from http://people.bu.
    edu/  wwildman/WeirdWil dWeb/ courses/
    mwt/ dictionary/methemes; Internet.

Slick, Mat, (n.d.) 2014 Are there apostles for
    today? Christian Apologetics and
    Research Ministry. Retrieved from:
    http://carm.org/

The Christian Faith. H.R. Mackintosh
    and J.S. Stewart, eds. London: T & T Clark,
    1999.

Smith, Alanzo H., and J Smith "Parishioner
    Attitudes Toward the Divorced/Separated:
    Awareness Seminars as Counseling
    Interventions." In Counseling & Values, no.
    45 (October 2000).

Thomas-Living Right in a Wrong World: 2012
September 2012. Retrieved from thomas-
livingrightinawrongworld.blogspot.com/2012_0
9_01_archive.ht..


Vassiliou, George A."Analogic Communications
    as a Means of Joining the Family System in
    Therapy." International Journal of Family
    Psychiatry, no. 4 (2003).

Williams, Colin W. John Wesley's Theology
    Today. 1960 Nashville, TN: Abingdon Press,

William, M. (n.d). Mysterious apostle and his
    legacy, not  easily defined. Washington
    Times, The(DC).

Williams, Roger and David C. Ruesink. "The Changing Rural Family ... and Community: Implications for Congregational Ministry." In Family Ministry (Winter 1998).

Witski, Steve. "A Preliminary Defense of Prevenient Grace" In The Arminian Magazine, vol. 18 no. 2 (Fall, 2000); Retrieved from http://www. fwponline.cc/v18n2witzki.ht ml;

Wommack, A. (2015) Paul's Thorn in the Flesh. Retrieved from http://www.awmi.net/extra/article/paulsthorn

Selah!